Seasons of Play

Seasons of Play

Natural Environments of Wonder

Rusty Keeler

Gryphon House
www.gryphonhouse.com

Published by Gryphon House, Inc.
P. O. Box 10, Lewisville, NC 27023
800.638.0928; 877.638.7576 (fax)
Visit us on the web at www.gryphonhouse.com.

Bulk Purchase
Gryphon House books are available for special premiums and sales promotions as well as for fund-raising use. Special editions or book excerpts also can be created to specifications. For details, call 800.638.0928.

Disclaimer
Gryphon House, Inc., and Rusty Keeler cannot be held responsible for damage, mishap, or injury incurred during the use of or because of activities in this book. Appropriate and reasonable caution and adult supervision of children involved in activities and corresponding to the age and capability of each child involved are recommended at all times. When making choices about allowing children to eat certain foods, plants, or flowers, make sure to investigate possible toxicity and consider any food allergies or sensitivities. If in doubt about safety, do not ingest food or plants. Whenever children are near fire or flames, they must be supervised carefully. Do not leave children unattended at any time. Observe safety and caution at all times.

Library of Congress Cataloging-in-Publication Data
Names: Keeler, Rusty, author.
Title: Seasons of play : natural environments of wonder / Rusty Keeler.
Description: Lewisville, NC : Gryphon House, Inc., [2016] | Includes index.
Identifiers: LCCN 2016005228 (print) | LCCN 2016017342 (ebook) | ISBN
  9780876596128 (pbk.) | ISBN 9780876596135 (e-book)
Subjects: LCSH: Play environments—Design and construction. | Plants for play
  environments. | Playgrounds—Design and construction. |
  Playgrounds—Environmental aspects. | Physical education for children.
Classification: LCC GV425 .K44 2016 (print) | LCC GV425 (ebook) | DDC
  790.06/8—dc23
LC record available at https://lccn.loc.gov/2016005228

Contents

Part 1

The Children and the Yards

Part 2

Construction Projects
and Resources

Preface

Every child deserves . . .

- Every child deserves a safe place to play.
- Every child deserves supportive adults watching him grow.
- Every child deserves an environment that offers her endless possibilities.

Your children can have that. Your outdoor space can support that. You can be a part of it.

The environments in this book are not overly complex, expensive, or hard to build. The spaces were built by hand by teachers, friends, and families. One was built all at once. One evolved over time. All of them continue to grow and change and always will. Just like children.

The environments in this book are successful for the preschoolers and families they serve. What works in one center might not work in another school. Each child's needs are unique. Everyone's situation is different. Some outdoor areas are shady, and some are sunny—that affects what plants you can grow. Some are used by lots of children at once, and others may be used by small groups of children. Some yards need to handle wild, rambunctious, high-energy children, and some schools have mellow explorers and gardeners. What are your children like? What do they need? How can you create opportunities to explore and challenge and grow?

Another name for this book could be *A Year in the Life of the Natural Playscape.* It is a window to the natural-play environment and a glimpse at what happens there, what children do, what adults say "yes" to, and what natural spaces for children can look and function like—in all seasons, all year long. I hope what you'll see will inspire you to think about your own outdoor spaces in new ways. I hope you get ideas for changes you can make to your yards—plants you could add, paths you could build, gardens you could grow. Little by little, step by step. Big changes can happen with small additions over time.

I also hope you get ideas for changes you can make in yourself and how you use your outdoor space and what you allow children to do. The creation of a natural play space is part of it; the other part is you. What do you allow your children to do outside? When do you let them go out? For how long? In what kinds of weather? With what kinds of freedoms and with what kinds of loose parts to use? Some of the scenes in this book may surprise you. Children digging—everywhere. Children making a mess. Children outside in winter. Children playing with water outside in winter!

As you look, I hope you reflect on your own sense of self in your yard with your children. What do you say "yes" to? What do you say "no" to? Are there new activities you can let the children try? Are there new ways for you to be in the yard that allow children new freedoms and opportunities to explore, challenge, and grow, and more fully inhabit the natural yard you create?

Can you help them feel free to be?

Introduction

Hello!

This book is a window to the world of natural outdoor environments for young children.

A few summers ago, I started a project that is now the book you are holding. I teamed up with some of my favorite local home-based preschools to document the amazing things that happen in their backyards in different seasons. Outdoor play and learning is an important part of each center's educational philosophy, and they each have a very cool—and very different—natural playscape backyard.

- One space is a garden playscape oasis in the city with fruit trees, a sand pit, vegetable garden, grassy areas, and a hill.
- One space is a wild, rough-and-tumble jumble of plants, logs, sand, and dirt.
- One space is a minifarm with chickens, goats, cats, and a pony on a large, sloped yard with loose parts and hand-built play pieces.

Each space is amazing, with beautiful opportunities for children to be children and with freedom and support for play. I love seeing children inhabit a natural space, make it their own, and live fully in the present moment with their world. In my world, these yards have all the good stuff—leaves, apples, sand, flowers, kale, grass, rocks, mud, and more.

I am honored to have been witness to so many beautiful moments in these yards.

I am delighted to share them with you.

I hope you get lots of ideas for your own yard!

Part 1

The Children and the Yards

The Seed Center

Jacquelyn Beuchel, director
Eight children, three to six years old

The outdoor space at the Seed Center is one of the sweetest back yards on the planet. Built with love and care by Jacquelyn and her husband, Aaron, this space has a multitude of sweet little features thoughtfully created and placed within a small lot in the city. When Aaron and Jacquelyn moved in, the yard was flat, open, and totally exposed to the adjacent parking lot and buildings. They installed an attractive wooden fence for instant privacy and began playscaping the yard and preparing it for children's play and exploration. In went gardens, paths, shrubs, sand pits, raised planters, a hill and hill slide, stone, grass, wood chips, and much more. It is truly a natural oasis in the city.

Summer

Late summer. Green grass,
green leaves on trees.
Harvest time in the garden:
tomatoes, basil, squash, kale.
Harvest time in the miniorchard: apples!

Playscape Plants

People often wonder what kinds of plants are best for children's playscapes. I love what they did here: vegetable plants as playscape plants! What a neat idea. Pathways cutting through kale forests! A Brussels sprout jungle! So cool, and makes so much sense. We know vegetables are safe to eat. Go ahead and nibble, kids. Edible playscape!

Garden

Loading your playscape with multisensory plants is a great way to safely add tasting to your yard. But this doesn't mean you have to be timid in your plant selections. This garden has cherry tomatoes, cucumbers, and lettuce, but it also has abundant nasturtiums! Have you ever eaten those? Spicy! But it's good to mix things up. Let kids experience it all for themselves. Children might not like the spicy plants—ouch!—but they might. Maybe they will develop a taste for spicy stuff. Or maybe they'll just use the brightly colored flowers for potions. Plants as play props. Plant material as loose parts. Without telling anyone, Jacquelyn snuck stevia, which could be the sweetest plant alive, into the garden. Only the nibblers will discover it. But when they do, look out! Those sweet leaves will get gobbled up quicker than you can say, "Shoo Peter Rabbit, shoo!"

Tepee Corner

The elements in this yard were fun not just for children but for the adults who built them, too. This sweet tepee spot is filled with more great playscape plants, such as Jerusalem artichokes (tall, fast-growing, prolific, hardy, edible tubers), kale (nice texture, edible cooked and raw), butterfly bush (a wildlife attractor), a small rose bush (fragrant flowers), and forsythia (early marker of spring with bright yellow flowers).

Hard Surface

A paved area is perfect for bikes, trikes, wagons, and balls.

Messy Area

It's always great to have spaces—big or small—where children can create, construct, sort, stack, and make a mess. This "anarchy zone" corner is filled with natural loose play elements such as pine cones, rocks, leaves, pine needles, and pebbles. Endless possibilities for fairy huts, house building, dramatic play, and more.

Apples! Apples! Apples!

Once again: edible playscape. At this time of
year, the apples are ripe and ready for picking and
chomping. Every activity seems to be accompanied
by the sweet flavor of apples. Crunch!

Hillside Slide

A hill slide is a great way to get down a hill
quickly—or to launch a rolling apple.

Another Apple, Please

What flavor am I in the mood for? A Red Delicious? A big Granny Smith? I think I'll try them all and then decide. Thank you, Jacquelyn!

Sand Play

Big work happening in the sand pit. Big boulders hold the sand in place. Shovels, trucks, and construction toys help children dig into their world. Brrrrrum, brrrrrrum!

Apple Tree Climb

Up, up, up you go! Test your strength. Follow your instincts. Listen to the tree. Trust your intuition.

   Should children climb trees? Of course! Can adults find ways to feel comfortable allowing them to climb? Yes. Clip pokey branches; talk to children about climbing safety and not going too high; and spread soft wood chips beneath the tree.

Hills

Roll down a hill. Over and over again.

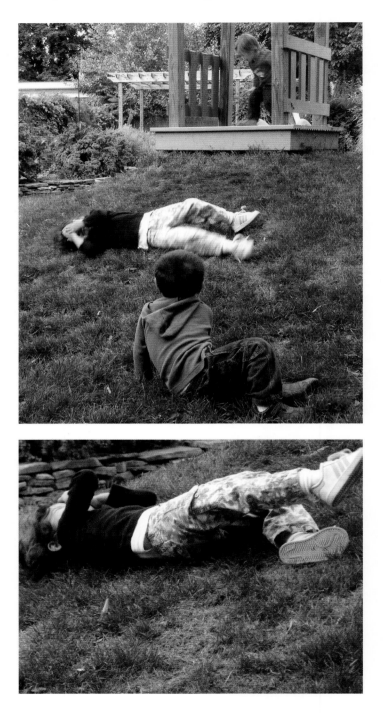

Autumn

Another beautiful time of the year.
Things are changing. Leaves are
turning. Late-harvest vegetables are
now ready. The air becomes crisp.
Cooler temperatures. Requires some new
layers of clothing. Sweatshirt time!

Leaf Pile

What wonders await in the raked pile of leaves? What ever could a child do here?

Whee!

In we go. Over and over. Then toss them in the air.

Up in the Air

Watch the leaves fly and float and flutter. Grab a crunching
handful and throw them up again. What does it look like?
How does it feel? The essence of the season. Celebration time.

In a Bed of Leaves

Eyes closed, calm. Quiet rustle. The world stops;
the action changes. A soft place to be.

Seasonal Snapshots

Kale growth galore!
Burning bushes burning red.
A scattering of brown
leaves, rain barrel full from
recent storm. Ready for new
challenges with the hill slide.

Winter

"There's no bad weather, just bad clothing."

Get Ready

Get those clothes on! Layer up—hats, gloves, coats, boots, snow pants, and scarves. Teachers, too. Sunny day but still cold out.

World Transformed

The power of precipitation! It's just cold water, but what a difference it makes to your place and play. Wide-eyed wonder. At first, just go out and see what's what. Then how about a nibble of some snow or ice? Yum!

Trudge, Trudge

Arctic explorers, bundled and bulky, stomping, stopping, in the soft white world.

Tepee Time

Gotta investigate the tepee hut hideaway. The green plants are long gone, but the stalks still remain. Pick, pluck. A reed or rod becomes an explorer's ski pole, a snow poker, a staff. Stop and see what the snow can do. What does it look like, how does it feel as it crumbles?

Stuck!

A snow storm will do that. Cover you up. Blanket your stuff. Hidden trike unearthed, shoveled out, still stuck.

Cover Me in Snow

Like at the beach except different! Shovel loads and handfuls of snow.
Answer children's pleas to "bury me!" Peaceful giggles.
What snowsuits were made for.

Magic Droplets

Beautiful moments of discovery. Keeping perspective, adults saying yes, yes. Drips on your head. Drops on your hand. Wet hands, wet coat, wet head. Wonderful!

Spring

New life! New season. New chance to
get outside. Feel the sun, feel the green.
Soak it up. Spirits soaring. Sprouts rising up.
Tend the garden. Celebrate the renewal.

Sunny Spring

So good to get outside! Feeling the season with all the senses. Fresh green growing. Tepee ready for another season. Plant stalks trimmed and ready for new growth. Apple trees bursting with beautiful blossoms. The air is filled with sweet fragrance.

Fresh Green

Nibble, nibble. Tastes good.
Fresh green kale sprouting
from stalks that survived the
winter. Yum!

Water

Water, water, plenty of water
to water.

Watering

What's growing this time of year in the garden? Kale and garlic.
Give them water. Help them grow.

Spring Snapshots

The beauty of slides: many adventurous ways up and down.
Rain barrel fills a watering can.
Kid nest on stone wall beside dandelion.
Beneath the blossoms.

Garden Gifts

More gardening activities. Water those new plants. And look at seeds now sprouting in cups. Spray them gently with water. Soon they will be ready for transplant.

Rain Barrel Water Gathering

Freedom to fill the basin. Freedom to watch water.
Caregiver nearby, but trusting, allowing. And with that,
learning by doing, watching, observing. Splashes in patterns
of the universe. Sounds of dribbles. Fill your watering can,
pour it out with a friend. Moments in time.

Fresh Blossoms

Apple tree is a friend all year long. Spring seems like the most beautiful season. Back in the tree we go!

Summer Again

Easy living in the summertime. Hot, but shady spots beckon. Picnic weather, water-play weather, ice-play weather! Exploring the green and the good life.

Cold Ice, Hot Day

Blocks of ice. Food coloring and salt make surprising patterns. Melt magic.

Fabric Silks

Strong fabric swaths tied to trees provide gathering spots, cozy nap nooks, swaying swings, and more. Once again: thank you, apple trees!

Swing to Sand

Shoes off, rockabye cradle.
Shoes off, squish in the sand.

Summer Snapshots

One beauty of a natural playscape is that you can try new things every year.
Change it up. A thousand experiments! Try new things. A living space.
Last summer kale forests; this summer a Jerusalem artichoke tunnel with more
stepping-stone work. Flurries of flowers, all different plants. The world begins
anew. No tepee this year but an enclosed bamboo fence beside the tall plantings.
Shelter of another sort. Rain barrel beside full-blown basils and mint.

Outdoor Art

The perfect place to get messy. Plop some paint. Hey, wasn't that big wooden spool used in the anarchy corner last year? Yup! That's the beauty of nonfixed play pieces: just like devising new planting plans or classroom layouts, loose parts can be moved and altered and used in a variety of different ways and locations.

Apple Roll

Apples as loose play props. Gather them from the ground. There's way more apples here than can be eaten. What happens when you put them on a slide? Chutes away! Going the distance. Going for speed. Again and again.

Picnic Place

Eating outside.
Fresh air,
friends, food, fun.
Wish you were here!

Seed Center Yard Plan

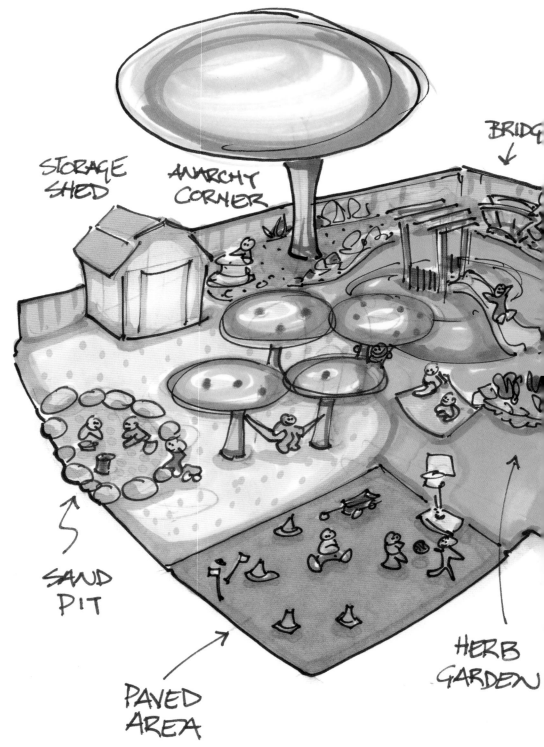

STORAGE SHED

ANARCHY CORNER

BRIDG

SAND PIT

PAVED AREA

HERB GARDEN

SEED CENTER

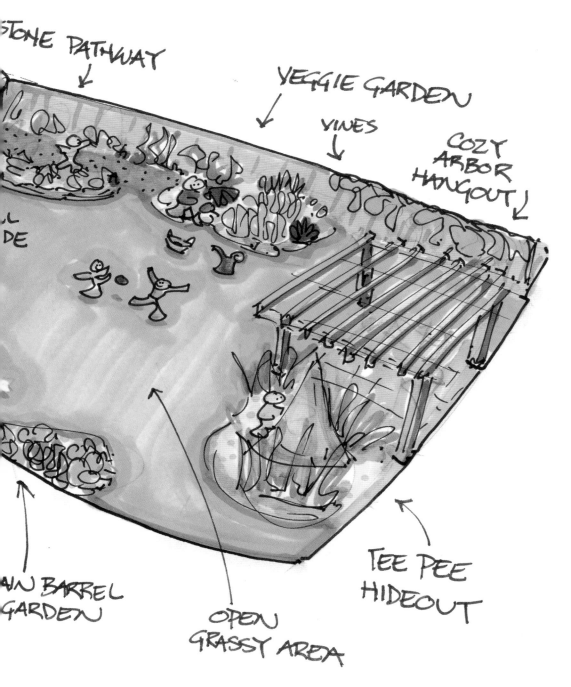

STONE PATHWAY

YEGGIE GARDEN

VINES

COZY
ARBOR
HANGOUT

...OL
...DE

...AN BARREL
GARDEN

OPEN
GRASSY AREA

TEE PEE
HIDEOUT

A Conversation with Jacquelyn Beuchel, Director of the Seed Center, and Her Husband, Aaron

Rusty: What attracted you to the idea of nature play and playscapes?

Jacquelyn: As a kid I was always outside in the yard or going on hikes with my parents. We went camping all the time. I have three brothers, so we were always outside building roads in the yard with trucks. I liked being outside, and I really love gardening. And I love sharing gardening with kids.

Aaron: Same for me—growing up in California there was a lot of open space. My brother and I would go down to the creek and lose track of time. We'd spend hours down there damming it up or racing sticks or whatever. And also for aesthetic reasons: it's our house, we live here. We like to garden and have a nice yard, and the idea of starting a preschool and dumping a whole bunch of plastic toys out back definitely didn't seem right.

Jacquelyn: I think it's more calming for children to have natural playscapes than the plastic ones.

Aaron: And I just think it looks junky when you look at places that have all that plastic stuff out there. It gets old and mildewy, the plastic fades....

Jacquelyn: Right. And then you have to deal with it when you are done with it. When the plastic stuff breaks and cracks, it goes in the trash. Natural things break down naturally, or you can reuse them in a different way.

Aaron: You can re-create everything that you could do on a traditional playground with natural materials. You can have a wall for balancing on, and you can climb or swing from trees.

Jacquelyn: I like the rock wall because it's natural and uneven. Balance beams are straight and always the same, so your footing is always the same. But on the rock wall, the rocks wiggle and that's actually really good for kids working on their balance.

Aaron: I've seen studies that looked at natural playscapes and safety and how on a traditional playground things are too predictable—the bars that you climb up are all the same distance apart for example—and it's actually more dangerous in a way because it doesn't teach the kids to use their brain. Children actually learn balance and climbing better when things are not standardized. They have to really focus. When I read that I was like, "Wow! This just makes so much sense."

Jacquelyn: And children can do so many things on the hill. They can slide on it, climb up, roll down. Or they could lay on it and just look at the clouds.

Aaron: And again, safety with the hill. Who is going to hurt themselves on a hill?

Rusty: How did you start your natural playscape project? What were your steps?

Aaron: The first thing was the hill and hill slide, probably because that's such a classic feature of a natural playground. We got the slide from a yard sale. Once we started going down that path, we began to find all kinds of stuff for the yard. A friend gave us a bunch of boulders that were left over from a contracting job. Then the massive sandbox. In some ways sand and water is all you need!

Jacquelyn: The sand pit is our favorite spot. Especially with shade from the apple trees right there.

Aaron: You have to think of all those things too. You can't stick a sandbox in hot sun, or else it's not going to get used as much. We also wanted kids to be able to climb the trees, so we mulched around them in case someone fell. We wanted to have some padding.

Jacquelyn: The apples are so great in so many ways. One time I remember a little boy separating the apples by size, large and small, into small tubs. That is a great skill to work on in pre-K. I did not ask him to do it; it was a natural thing. He decided he wanted to sort them. Kids just naturally know what they need to work on.

Rusty: And the environment provided the stuff....

Jacquelyn: That's right. It was just the apples that fell on the ground. Another time children were making a "stew" out of the apples, and they were making it on the far side of the yard in the pergola. All the kids were doing it. It started out with two, and they were running back and forth carrying buckets of water from one side of the yard to the other. I could have said, "Oh you can take this project closer to the water." But the running was so good, and they had time to think about what they were doing. Kids need a lot of planning time and wait time. So they thought it was pretty cool. They were making the stew over there, and they were getting some of the vegetables from the garden, and some apples, and water from the water pump. So they would get water and then carry it over, and someone was stirring. They all had jobs, and they knew what they were doing. It just happened. It's pretty awesome.

Rusty: How about the actual construction of the playscape? Did you do all the work yourselves? Did you have people to do it? How did that go?

Aaron: We had some help. We had Jen (the assistant teacher) and her husband helping with the initial building of things like the hill and moving the boulders for the sandbox. We used PVC pipes as a little trolley system for the bigger ones. We moved the rocks one by one, inch by inch. That was fun!

We were finding things for the preschool everywhere—online, garage sales, school auctions.

Rusty: Did you have a big vision to start with and build it in phases, or did you just do it as inspiration hit?

Aaron: In terms of construction, it wasn't a big production. We just sort of chipped away at it. Like the hill slide. That's was just dumping a big pile of dirt and then raking it out and throwing grass seeds at it. It wasn't hard at all.

Our partner Jen's husband was a landscape architect, and he took our ideas and put them down on a plan and gave us a vision.

Rusty: How long from when you first started building it until everything was in place? Was it years?

Aaron: No. It was fast. We did it in one summer.

Rusty: One of the things I love about the space is that it always continues to evolve. It is always different over time.

Aaron: Yeah. We wanted to go with the seasons. When it's fall, what do you have at hand? Do you have a lot of leaves? And what's more fun than jumping in a pile of leaves? In winter, we get a lot of snow and ice.

Jacquelyn: Winter was interesting because we had a lot of days where things would turn into ice. Some of the yard was icy, some of it was slushy. And each was a different kind of experience.

The kids would use the sticks from the Jerusalem artichokes. They made tepees. They were fishing with them and doing all different things—things I would never have thought of. I remember something that I think I heard from Bev Bos—when a kid is doing something, you ask yourself, "Why not? Why can't he do it?" So I often would say that to myself when they were working on something. "Why can't I let them do that? Is there a reason? Is it because I don't want it messy? Or is it unsafe? What is the real reason?" So I think it is good to ask yourself when kids are working, exploring, and getting messy, "Why can't they do it?" I like when kids get messy.

You want opportunities for some safe risk. Bev Bos also talks about "the illusion of risk" and having success. Children need to be risk takers to help build critical thinking skills. If a child is working on something at school and they feel like they can't do it, they might stop. But if they have experienced taking risks and overcoming them, then they might try different things. It teaches them to more confidently problem solve.

Rusty: What do parents think of your yard? Do you have to explain certain things to them about your yard and what their children will be doing out there?

Jacquelyn: Parents really love it. They are always drawn to the yard. I tell them we might get messy because some parents are not okay with that. Our school didn't really have parents like that, but I know some other parents don't like their kids to get dirty.

Aaron: She has to manage parents' expectations for cleanliness. Let them know not to send children here in their nicest clothes.

Jacquelyn: Right. In preschools, children need to get messy, painting and everything. I had one little boy go to the sandbox and just lay in it when it was wet. He needed that sensory experience. His mom understood that that is what he needed, and she was okay with it. That was so beautiful.

Rusty: How about the health inspectors or the licensing folks? Did you have to convince them?

Jacquelyn: Oh, they loved the yard. Seriously!

Aaron: Our licensor did not have any problems with the climbing of trees or anything like that, right?

Jacquelyn: He just said to make sure we had mulch on the ground under the trees. And tomatoes had to be behind the fence because the leaves are toxic to eat.

Rusty: Were there any specific challenges you had to overcome? Things about the yard, certain plants to grow, the way kids use the space, or stuff that people might be worried about?

Jacquelyn: You have to be careful when you are planting things, and then the kids want to run in the garden. You just have to talk to the kids about it. Our children are pretty good. They can see where the path is. Sometimes they forget, but I think that plants are usually pretty healthy.

Aaron: Choosing durable plants is important!

Jacquelyn: Make sure that you plant the right things in the areas you think they might jump through.

Aaron: Once kale gets going, it's pretty hard to hurt. It's a tough plant.

Jacquelyn: When kids are involved in the planting, then they are more invested and protective of the plants. They worked hard planting the seeds, watched them grow, and then we put them outside. Kids who don't normally eat those sorts of things will eat them because they feel the plant is part of them.

Aaron: Another thing you can do is just bring stuff from outside and dump it in your sensory table inside.

Jacquelyn: If it's too cold outside, bring snow in. I've had dirt in the sensory table, or sticks and leaves because we were gardening. One time they made stick-mud birthday cakes. We take playdough outside, and they make prints of everything in the yard. I like to mix the two areas, inside and outside.

Rusty: What advice do you have for people wanting to do a natural playscape?

Aaron: It doesn't take a lot of money. You just need to find materials. It could be a tree, a stump, or whatever.

Jacquelyn: You could get stumps from someplace and let the kids walk on them, sit on them. Or you could make a little sitting area. The kids will figure out what to do with them. They can roll them around the yard. A tepee is always a good place to start. Kids love that.

Aaron: It doesn't have to be superextravagant. It can just be simple stuff that you put out there. Then kids will probably figure out uses that you didn't even think of. If it's something they can move, that is probably even better. Just keep it kind of loose and supply the materials.

Aaron: What other advice?

Jacquelyn: Start small. Work with what you have in your yard. Kids don't need a lot, really. They have great imaginations!

Corner of the Sky

Valerie Akers, director
Twelve children, three to six years old

Compared to the pristine playscape garden at the Seed Center, the outdoor play yard at Corner of the Sky is a mess! But that doesn't make it any less appealing and interesting for children. The stuff that goes on here is fabulous. The play here can be rough and tumble, but the yard can take it. It's rugged too. It's a place where children can range free. Build up, drag around, trample, tend, dig, protect, discover, enjoy, investigate, imagine, be. A real kid habitat.

Summer

Late summer. Shady green still holding on. Warm days, dry. Dusty. Shrubs have leaves, act as screens, and create areas for hiding and hanging out.

Wild Flat Lands

Stepping-stones in dirt lead you directions. Stumps, planting beds, sprays of grasses and herbs popping up here and there. Seating, work tables, natural materials. Picked leaves become an oversized sensory table salad.

Players in Place

Feeling at home in their natural habitat. Free to roam, hang out,
be yourself. Plants surround, create shapes and spaces to be.

Wonderings

What's in the bush? Do you see it, too?
Keep looking, keep looking. A bug?
A bird's nest? A flower bulb?

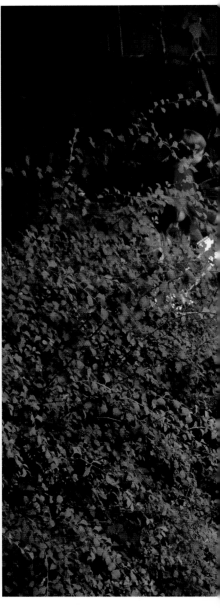

Dusty Cityscape

I don't see any lawn here. No grass anyway. Doesn't seem to matter!
It's all still happening. And more. . . You can't really shovel rows
and roads in grass with snow shovels can you? And look here—
a rake toll gate. "What's the magic word?" "Please?"
"That's it. Go ahead."

Tin-Can Orchestra

Spoons on metal. Bang-bang-bang. Shovel off that table, clean
it up. And back to bang-bang-bang. Add in an electronic guitar?
Stay centered, teacher Val! Breathe. . . .

Gliding through Space

Loose parts lend possibilities.
Pick 'em up and move them.
Place them. Replace them.
Set up and sail.

More Spoon Pan Drumming

Stumps as tables, as drum kit with multiple levels and sounds.
With bells tied up. Ding-a-ling.

Move the Sound Around

Loose instruments can go anywhere. Bring it to the bench.
Gather around. Play together. Make more sound.

Spoon Tunes

Metal spoons, metal bowls, and baking trays. As simple as that when adults say "yes." Getting into it! Hit those pans! Bang it out!

More Searching

Looking behind tufts of fuzzy grass. More plants. Herbs, mints.
Give it a sniff. Slow paced, inquisitive, focused.

Inviting You

Corner hideout. Hang behind shrubs. Hit the main entrance, or loop around back on logs.

Work to Be Done

Hard hats, shovel excavators, sound effects.
Earth moving!

Shovel It Up

Shovel that dirt. Kick up that dust.
Take a breather, then back to work.

Loose Stuff Happens

Handful of dust into the bowl.
Stir it up. Trucks back up and
dump. Bands of children work and
wander. Sidewalk between houses
leads to streets and beyond.

Gather Around

There's a sandpit under that tarp. But for now a great place
for group gatherings. Sit around, discuss.

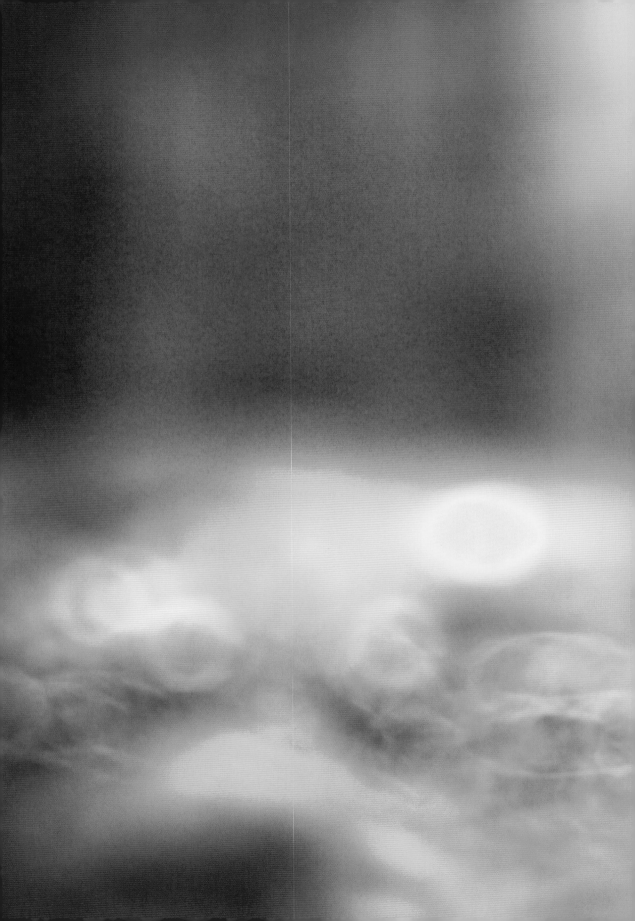

Autumn

Something new in the air. Worlds transform.
Only the hardy plants survive. Pumpkin time.
Cider time. Crunchy leaves time.

First Frost

Overnight cold snap crunches leaves, knocks out the delicates. Many garden plants die. End of tomatoes. Frost clinging to the collapsed leaves. But that's okay—it's another moment in the life of children and the outside world.

Driftwood Fort

Beautiful natural structure built by kids and adults. Driftwood from the lake lashed together with twine. Beans and flower vines growing up and over. Reaching around, greening it up. Bells hung inside for extra sensory twinklings.

Plants through Seasons

Even crunchy, scraggly plants can create spots to be,
places to play, backdrops to daily life.

Covered Sand Pit

Love the round mirror, loose parts galore. Stumps, branches, sticks.
And also pots, pans, sifters, spoons, bowls, bins, rakes, chalk.
Perfectly stored beside the sand—right where you need them.
Nothing purchased new. Hand-me-down dishes, secondhand silverware.

In the Flow

Looking for bugs. Then superheroes fighting bad guys.
Then stopping to spot a bean pod.

Chime Railing

Twinkle, twinkle as you head up and down the stairs.
Homemade metal work attached to steps. Sounds as you
enter and exit the yard.

Gateway in Autumn

Leaves browning, flowers gone, vines now crunchy.

Winter

Ah, winter—crisp and pristine. But late
winter, not a pretty time. Snow patches
remain here and there. Cold! Winter still has
a grip, but small signs of spring are popping
up if you know where to look (or dig or rake).

Sprouts!

Look closely among the cold, leafless, brown bushes: New life! Green! Could spring be just around the corner? Tulip leaves, crocuses. Protect those sprouts with tiny barricades. Mini-stockade fences. Protect against trampling by ferocious plastic dinosaurs.

Multiple Personalities

Free to be. Relaxing spots, funny faces. Rake the leaves to find what is revealed beneath.

Color among Brown

Always good to have resting spots to plop
down, chill out, take it all in. Crunch of leaves.
Crisp of air. Sparkling treasure found and
stored in a sea of brown and gray.

Winter Stuff

Loose play parts are still there for the using.
Everything weatherproof and durable.
Strong against elements—and kids!

Wagon Rides

Teacher-powered wagon adventures. Follow the trail.
Hit the mud. Pass through the tunnel. Help from behind.
Friends packed into shared experience.

Glove Pile

It's okay to not wear gloves sometimes, even
when it's cold out. Trusting children to know
and make those decisions.

Moveable and Muddy

Sturdy stuff can be used all year. Traffic cones, shovels.
Melting snow reveals buried stones. Every day is different.

Spring

Sun again! Warm again! Green again!
Feels good to be back out with life growing
and spring energy flowing.

Corner Nook Revisited

Bushes back with leaves. A new driftwood-tree-branch structure
has appeared, making this passageway more elegant, regal.
Planned and built by kids and adults. Pass through proper!

Back in Action

Log places to sit. Adventurers gathering.
Seeking treasure!

Finding Flowers

Interested in seeing spring flowers? Come along. He'll show you. Check it out.

Sweet Lilac

Ah, the smells, smells, smells, and colors of spring—bathing the yard in scents and scenes.

Tulips

See, tulips. Flowers, blooming. Beheld.

Moods and Make Believe

Places to exist, to be, to feel, to express, to exclaim.

Snapshots

Lilac tunnels in bloom. Lashed branch structure leaning, leaning. Shadows and light, child-sized forest. Sitting around the sand-pit benches.

143

Gem Hunt around the Lilacs

Marbles and gems sprinkled around the yard. Search and discover!

Happy Loose Parts

Loose logs, branches, bark, tea pots. With smiling faces nearby. . . .

CORNER OF THE SKY

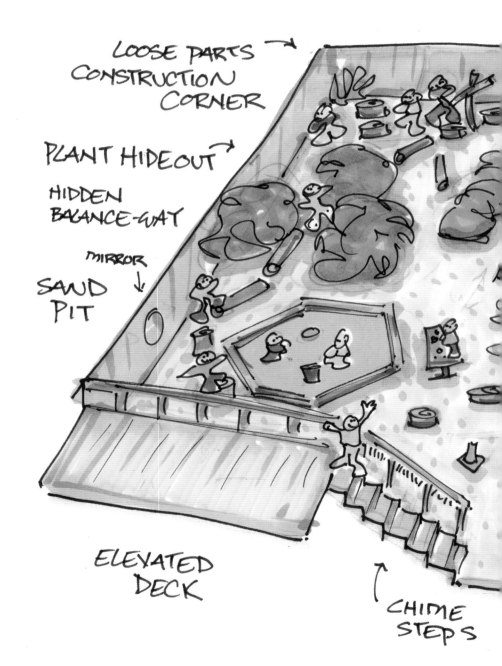

LOOSE PARTS
CONSTRUCTION
CORNER

PLANT HIDEOUT

HIDDEN
BALANCE-WAY

MIRROR

SAND
PIT

ELEVATED
DECK

CHIME
STEPS

Corner of the Sky Yard Plan

RAISED
VEGGIE
BEDS

PLANTERS

LILAC
TUNNEL

DRIFT
WOOD
HUT

STEPPING
STONES

ENTRANCE
GATE

Insights from Valerie Akers, Director of Corner of the Sky

Boyville

Though the children's play space is the backyard of my house, I'd long ago let go of the notion that it was ever really mine. Every spring when the sprouts made their treacherous trek upward, I'd remind myself that I was growing children, not flowers. This is a space for experiments and exploration. It's a space for imagination. For bus rides and learning to take turns. For lion cages, and learning how to address one's fear of someone roaring loudly. And it's a space for families of all possible configurations. This is a space for active, hands-on learning, and my role is to witness their natural inclinations, and support and enhance those as best I can.

The year that Rusty documented Corner of the Sky was a unique one. It was the first and only time we began a school year with all boys. One brave girl did join us before the winter set in, but we started that fall in "Boyville." And because of that, I came face-to-face with many of my own biases as to what Boyville would look like. As so often is the case in a world inhabited by preschoolers, I was pleasantly surprised by what I learned.

Worker Guys

This fall was no exception. My desire for a certain backyard aesthetic had little to do with their desire to be "worker guys," and with only silent protests on my part we moved into a world ruled by the worker guys. One of the dads had donated his office's old blueprints. So daily, we'd tape one to the outside table and "the boss" (yes, our worker-guy world had a self-chosen boss, and no one challenged this) would collect the large glass jewels that were strewn about the yard and place them on the particular locations that the work was to take place. They'd all gather around for instruction, in a rowdy circle of orange worker-guy hats. After their plans were determined, they'd fill the wagon with shovels, rakes, and construction cones, and set up a work site.

And everything became a work site. The driftwood structures that we built around the yard were "fixed" to the point of being dismantled. The large stumps we had strenuously carried into the yard and exhaustingly buried deep enough for safely standing on were carved, cut, broken, and removed, leaving gaping holes to excavate and then fill up again —my request . . . safety first! This was our daily experience that fall, and it progressed with very little assistance from any of the teachers. Sometimes I would try to join them on the construction site, but they never liked my "worker-guy" voice, and I was left to wonder why I felt inclined to assume a worker-guy voice in the first place . . . did I mention my biases?!

The Yard

When I started the school in 2002, the backyard was a square of green grass. That spring we held our first Parent Work Day and built our large hexagonal sand box, two rectangular raised planters for flowers and vegetables, and a smaller square raised planter that became our herb garden. We bought two small lilac bushes and planted flowers all along the edges of the yard. By the third or fourth Parent Work Day we were asking parents to bring us any overstock from their yard, recognizing that spending money for flowers in a space ruled by children was a foolhardy endeavor, and that practice continues to this day. For the backyard, I buy twenty-five bags of sand two or three times a year, collect interesting used metal kitchen utensils for the sandbox (or the occasional parade that happens to pass through the yard), mesh bags of glass jewels that the "jewel fairy" sprinkles about when no one is looking, and kid-sized rakes and shovels that double as guitars when need be. The rest of our outdoor gear is donated. Most of the grass was gone after that first summer, so we began covering the ground in wood chips that we collect from the large pile the city makes after cutting down the local trees. This summer, several of my neighbor's trees were damaged in a storm, and when the tree cutters came to remove them, they agreed to give us a massive wood-chip mountain and several large sections of trunk.

Inside the classroom, I chose materials that were certain to be open-ended, yet carrying that same philosophy to the backyard proved more difficult for me. I struggled against my desire to keep the sand in the sandbox and other such nonsensical limitations. Perhaps it's because the changes to the outdoor space involve more large motor changes. Inside, everything can be put back after the children have finished playing, but sand rarely finds its way back to the sandbox and stumps cannot be fixed with wood glue. The alterations the children make in the yard are more irreversible, and reflect their sense of ownership.

Democracy

At Corner we do a lot of voting. At the start of each school year, we inform the children that the teachers make the rules regarding issues of safety but that all the other rules we will vote on together. And when we are outside, this voting occurs at our sandbox meetings. Anyone can call a sandbox meeting. We have a sandbox meeting bell, and once it's rung, everyone must stop what they are doing and come over to the sandbox. Whoever called the meeting lets us know what we are voting on and chooses the manner that we will vote. (For example: "Hands on your knees if you're ready to go in for lunch; hands on your back if you want five more minutes.") So sometimes it's decided that it's okay to pick the flowers and leaves; other times it is not. This fall we voted to remove all the edging stones from the gardens. Though moving them posed possible safety issues, we supported their desire to incorporate them into their play.

LittleLeaf

Priscilla Reyer, director
Eight children, three to six years old

This place is rootsy, rural, farmy, and has mixed
ages like a family. My son JJ attended this
school, and I loved him rubbing elbows with
chickens, sheep, baby lambs, straw bales, loose
parts, and mud. Learning the seasons through
life with livestock, children become trusted
caretakers and friends to animals. Plenty of
space to explore, dig, sled, and slide down.
The day of my visit was typical LittleLeaf winter
fun: snowsuit sledding, animal feeding and
watering, wandering explorations, egg gathering.

Winter

Life on the farm. Ice on the farm.
Animals, children, winter expeditions.
Snowsuit season. No reason to stay
inside. Explore!

Naptime, Then Outside

Rise and shine, put on your outside clothes. Get ready to explore beyond the colorful classroom walls.

Porch Patio

First stop just beyond the back door. Gather round, check it out.
Take in the day. See what's what.

Animal Friends

Animals help foster the spirit of love, connection, compassion, responsibility.

Ice-Block Experiments

Leave water outside overnight, and see what happens. Ice chunk!
Pour water, pour ice. Please touch. Please investigate!

Old-School Plaything

Built with care by parents of yesteryear. Reminders of tree houses,
hand-built forts. Simple design, simple challenges. Tied to hilltop tree.

Down to the Main Yard

Sit down and slide—look out below!

Rootsy Play + Chickens!

Hand-built tree swings are a natural playscape solution. Straw-bale spiral in the snow. Feeding food scraps to chickens and guinea fowl, watching as they gobble them up.

Caring for Livestock

Just like us, animals need food and water every day. Children help
manage the farm, and learn respect and responsibility for the animals.
The animals count on the children, and the children know it.

Balance Boards

Loose lumber and stumps create challenge.
Simple setup. Balance above the snow or
shark-infested waters. Don't fall off!

Chicken and the Egg

Happy highlight: children look for eggs.
Daily discovery! We feed chickens. Chickens feed us.

Sledding Sensation!

Slippery steep hill sets up prime sledding conditions—no sled needed! Over and over. On your bottom, on your belly. Feet first, face first. Joy, freedom, speed, soft landings. Laughter, smiles, soaring spirit, life memories made.

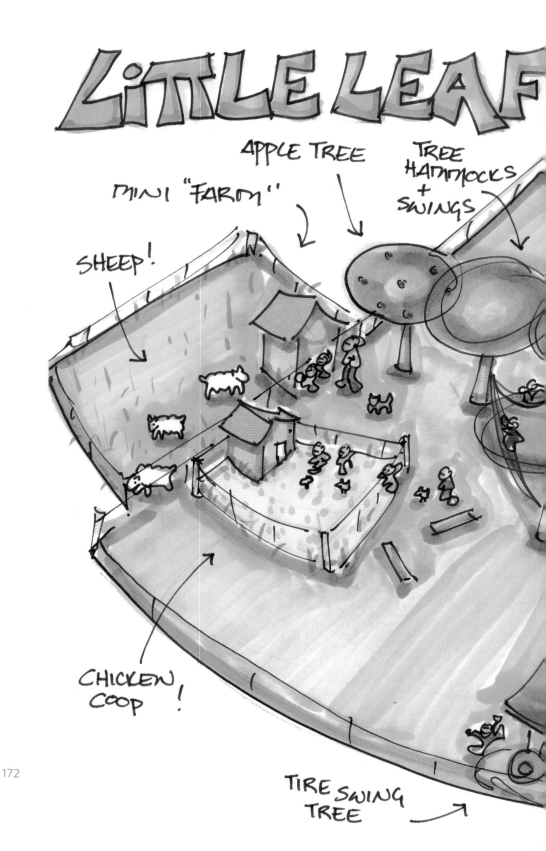

LITTLE LEAF

MINI "FARM"

APPLE TREE

TREE HAMMOCKS + SWINGS

SHEEP!

CHICKEN COOP!

TIRE SWING TREE

LittleLeaf Yard Plan

PLAY HUT LOOKOUT

UPPER DECK

...ANCE BOARDS

SLEDDING HILL

STRAW BALE SPIRAL

MAYPOLE TREE

SAND PIT

FIRE PIT

Ideas for Nature Play from Priscilla Reyer, Director of LittleLeaf Homestead School

One can never consent to creep when one feels an impulse to soar.
—Helen Keller, *The Story of My Life*

Free-Range Kids

Our outdoors space was designed with open and free-range exploration and play in mind. I wanted the children to feel free to roam, build, discover, hide, and creatively figure out their world. We have loose parts to build and create: tree stumps, garden carts, logs, buckets, hose access, ropes, sleds, sand, mud, and tools (rakes, hoes, shovels). There is a fire pit, a mud pit with a slide into it, trees to climb, hammocks to lie in and watch the clouds, swings to play on, hay bales to build with, a garden area, balance beams, and climbing structures.

Animals

Animals were always in the plan. We started with chickens. We used an incubator with fertile eggs donated from a couple of our students' homesteads. This was a beautiful connection between home and school life. The students created, planned, and built the chicken coop with the teachers. The chicks hatched during our school days. We cared for them in a brooder and eventually put them in the chicken coop. We used their eggs at snack time. We watched, year after year, as the hens hatched their own chicks. It was a miraculous circle that our children were able to witness, as most children attended for two to four years. Eventually, the children and teachers decided to have sheep at school. We discovered, measured, planned, and built a pasture for sheep. We cared for the animals every day: watering, feeding, petting, and taking on walks.

Safety

Safety is always a concern; when we teach and use communication skills effectively, the outdoors space is safe and engaging. The outdoors rules were that children had to be seen or heard by a teacher and be respectful. We practiced going into the woods, behind trees, and all throughout the yard looking, using hand signals, and shouting to be sure we were all within a safe distance. While tool use was monitored for safety, the children were always very mindful of their friends and surroundings. The yard was partially fenced due to a busy road and the neighbor's pond area. The rest of the play yard was open to the forest, meadows, and fields. Respectful behavior was all encompassing: feelings, nature, people, and animals.

Outside Activity

The children love being outdoors. Weather permitting—not freezing or raining too hard—we spend whole days out of doors. Naps, painting, crafts, lessons, and lunch in the sun, wind, or with the clouds. The children are disappointed when it's too cold to go outside!
As a director and teacher, I'm always doing reverent work while out of doors. I might be raking, sewing, knitting, fixing fences, organizing loose parts, digging, building, or caring for animals. I would always have children who were voluntary helpers and learners. Projects are also set up that children may take part in at any moment on their own while outside: felting, painting, woodwork, or seasonal crafts.

Sledding

For sledding, we station teachers at the top and bottom of the hill. On this day, the hill was slippery enough for children to go down without sleds with just a push from a teacher or a friend. For fun and safety, the children yelled out funny sayings like, "peanut butter antelopes!" and "pickle bunnies!" So we were all aware that a friend was ready to go down the hill and to be mindful. Look out below!

Part 2

Construction Projects and Resources

Construction Projects

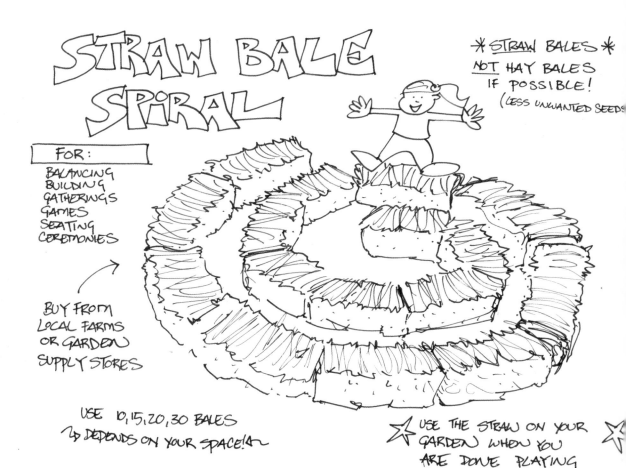

STRAW BALE SPIRAL

* STRAW BALES *
NOT HAY BALES
IF POSSIBLE!
(LESS UNWANTED SEEDS)

FOR:
BALANCING
BUILDING
GATHERINGS
GAMES
SEATING
CEREMONIES

BUY FROM
LOCAL FARMS
OR GARDEN
SUPPLY STORES

USE 10,15,20,30 BALES
↳ DEPENDS ON YOUR SPACE!↲

USE THE STRAW ON YOUR
GARDEN WHEN YOU
ARE DONE PLAYING

WINTER WINDCHILL PROTECTOR

BENCHES

OBSTACLE COURSE

RAISED PLANTERS

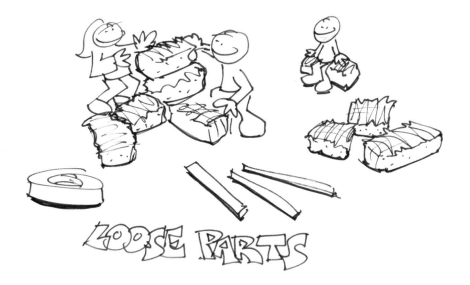

LOOSE PARTS

SAND PIT

ADD LOOSE PARTS
SHOVELS COOKIE SHEETS
SPOONS CUP CAKE TINS
BUCKETS MARBLES
PLASTIC DINOSAURS
TRUCKS

LANDSCAPE CLOTH

SIDE VIEW

BOULDERS

6" DEEP GRAVEL
(TO HELP WITH DRAINAGE)

SAND

GRAVEL

12-24" DEEP (OR MORE!)

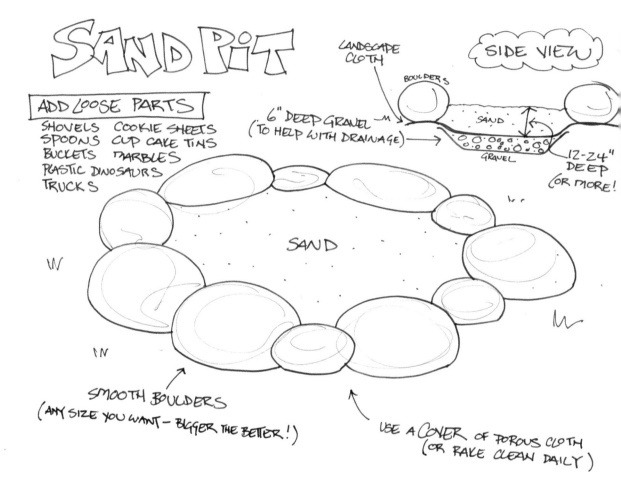

SAND

SMOOTH BOULDERS
(ANY SIZE YOU WANT — BIGGER THE BETTER!)

USE A COVER OF POROUS CLOTH
(OR RAKE CLEAN DAILY)

LOGS

DECK

TIMBERS

NO EDGING

PLANT HIDEOUT

BACK BALANCE/SITTING LOGS

PLASTIC MIRROR

SITTING LOGS

BACK ENTRANCE

STUMP BALANCE WAY

SCREENING SHRUBS

FRONT ENTRANCE

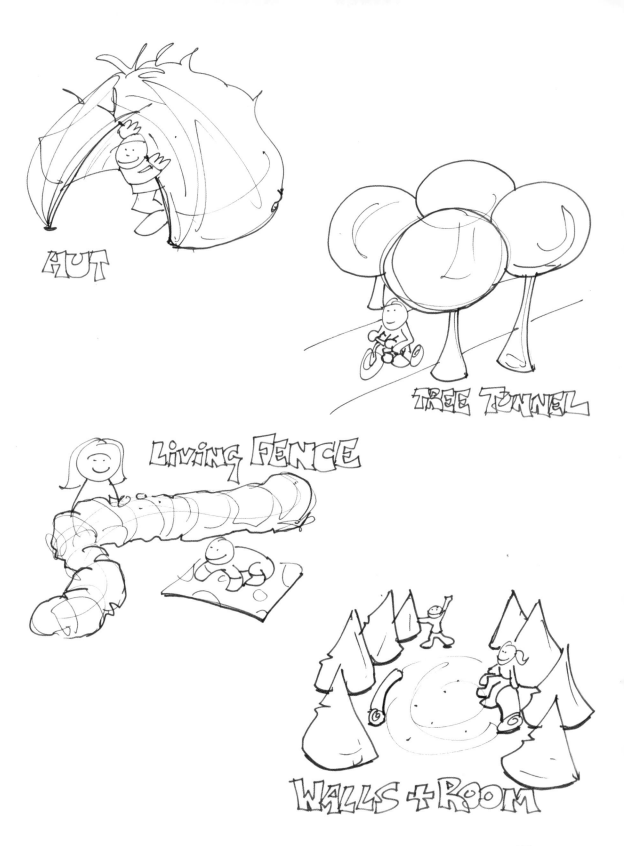

HUT

TREE TUNNEL

Living FENCE

WALLS + ROOM

Questions and Answers

*The questions and comments in bold came from members of the author's
EarthPlay Network Facebook group.*

**People often ask about whether to use treated or untreated timber in
playscape constructions.**
Good question! It all depends on what you are going to use the wood for and how long you
want it to last. Logs and stumps certainly don't need to be treated—let them rot and then
get more. Use whatever you can get your hands on. For wood in the ground though, like
fence posts and especially things like fixed play equipment, you need wood that will last
in the elements. I always try to use wood that is naturally rot resistant rather than wood
treated with chemicals. Well-known rot-resistant woods include cedar and black locust.
Depending on where you live, there may be other easily accessible woods. As a last resort—
or if the wood will be hidden and not able to be touched by children (like posts under a
deck)—I use treated wood. Treatments are less toxic than they used to be, and sometimes
it is very important to have wood that will not rot. (If you were building an arbor or a swing
set, for example.)

**How do you educate parents about risks? What are acceptable risks for
children in natural settings?**
Here are two great United Kingdom resources that talk about the benefits of risks for
children and walk you through the idea of weighing the benefits with the risks to make
informed and thoughtful decisions regarding your children's health, safety, and freedom to
play and explore:

http://www.hse.gov.uk/entertainment/childs-play-statement.htm
http://www.bathnes.gov.uk/sites/default/files/play_strategy.pdf

**Can you tell us more about how to get items donated for your playscape—
what kinds of places to go to, like tree-trimming services?**
There are so many ways to get help with your playscape project. People want to be a part
of good projects, especially fun projects for children—all you have to do is ask. First, make
a wish list of all the materials and people help you will need. Post it in a prominent place

where parents and staff will see it. Write a letter to the editor of the local newspaper talking about your project and listing the help and materials you'll need. Then think about people you know in your community and what skills they may have and how they may be able to help. Are there parents of your children with special skills? Staff? Relatives? Friends? Local community members? People who do carpentry, masonry, plumbing, gardening, fund-raising, PR, thank-you note writing, and cooking can all be a big help to your project. Artists, too! Make a list of what kinds of help you need and start asking. The same goes for materials for your playscape.

There are lots of places to get free stuff:

- Get wood chips, branches, or stumps from your local city forester or tree service business. Or if you see that a tree has blown down in your neighborhood after a storm, ask the landowners if you can chainsaw it up for your project.
- Ask for trees and shrubs from local nurseries or leftover plant materials from landscapers, contractors, golf courses, and orchards.
- Scout out boulders from local creeks or farms, or ask contractors who dig foundations. (They have to pay to get them hauled away. Tell them you'll take them off their hands for free!)
- Request scrap lumber from local contractors.
- Pick up used tires from tire shops (they are more than happy to give them away).
- Look for giant wood spools from cable companies or home supply stores.

How do you keep the playscape fresh and appealing as the years go by? (The kids do literally hundreds of sessions at the center, over the course of several years, and even the best-designed playground can get a bit humdrum with long-term familiarity.)
I hear you. Kids need a place where there are new possibilities every day, all year long. That's one of the beauties of a natural playscape vs. fixed play equipment—natural elements are always changing and growing (and dying). I think what makes a playscape fresh and appealing is the amount of fresh, appealing, and open-ended things kids can do out there—how much can the kids themselves change and alter the environment? (A sand pit with shovels and a water source never gets old.)

Can they dig in the dirt and mud? Can they play with water? Are there loose parts they can drag around? Can they build their own forts? Are there tools for them to use? Are there science instruments to help them investigate? The playscape itself is one part of the equation, but it's also about adults saying "yes" to kids creating, constructing, destroying, and discovering, and giving them the time and the materials to do so. Keep spicing it up. Keep looking for new strange loose parts to add to your yard. Get a storage shed and constantly curate the materials you provide for play.

You can also select plants that go through dramatic changes during the year. Vegetables, fruit trees, food plants! Flowers and flowering shrubs spruce up a yard. And how about animals! Never a dull moment with goats or chickens in the mix!

How do you keep newly planted trees and bushes alive when kids want to play among them as soon as possible?

I always recommend buying the largest and most established plants you can afford. The bigger and stronger the plant to start, the better. Some people rope off delicate plants as they get established. Other people use plants to ring the border of play areas, so they naturally act as fences or walls children don't automatically run through. I like that idea of thinking about running and play patterns and planting in and around them. (Some people wait to set path locations until they see where the wear and erosion happens, then make those spots the paths!) I've heard of people planting prickly plants to keep children from running through certain areas. Diabolical! (OK, I've done it a couple of times, I admit it.) Berry bushes can make nice borders and fences. I also recommend planting more of each plant than you normally would for your own residential backyard. Clump lots of shrubs together to make a wall. Plant a mini apple orchard instead of a single tree. They may grow into wild tangles after a couple years, but you'll know that they survived! (And tangles have aesthetic appeal too!)

Foraging for food. Is it worth doing or just too risky?

We all know how important and amazing it is for children to learn that food does not just come from grocery stores wrapped in plastic or fancy boxes—that fruits and vegetables grow in the ground, in the dirt. Amazing! And that kids themselves can be a part of the process of growing food. Beautiful! This thinking is part of the inspiration of the worldwide gardening for kids movement in schools, child care centers, and backyards! It's a meaningful opportunity for children to learn about plants and the cycles of the seasons and, in turn, how to be good stewards and caretakers of plants and gardens. But as you know, tended gardens are just one place where edible plants live. They also live in the wild. In nature. That's what the gatherers of hunter-gatherer societies gathered: wild foods in nature. Before we humans grew our food, we foraged for it. We knew what we were looking for, where to find it, and what time of year to gather it. Many people today love to forage for food and get truly excited over finding edible greens, berries, fruits, flowers, and mushrooms right in their own backyards and local wild lands. I have a secret patch of Chanterelle mushrooms that I giddily visit every July and gather to my heart's content. Delicious stuff! But I also know where there is a patch of "Destroying Angel" mushrooms that will kill you dead with a single bite. Yowch. So with foraging you gotta know your stuff. You gotta be able to identify your berries and mushrooms exactly. You need to know what leaves look like, colors, shapes, sizes of fruit. It all matters. It all makes a difference. Every plant has distinguishing characteristics that separate it from other plants. One purple berry makes a good snack. Another one can give you a belly ache.

So yes, foraging can be risky. It can be tricky. But does that mean you shouldn't do it? Like all things risky, it depends on your kids, your environment, and how comfortable you feel with the activity. Done with thoughtfulness and care, it can be a wonderful learning opportunity for children. A real teaching moment for you. It's important to teach that only certain plants are edible. That certain plants are poisonous. That certain plants can make you sick or worse. But at the same time that there are plants right in front of us, right in our yards that we can harvest for food or medicine. Maybe you can bring in a local expert to teach you and your children? Maybe you create an ongoing outdoor classroom project out of it. Bring in art. Study plant books. Draw the plant characteristics. It's real-life science for sure.

I say if it's something you already love to do, share it with your children. If it's something you're not comfortable with, don't do it. If it's something you're curious about trying, start small and safe. Here's a safe, small first-step foraging idea for you: Dandelions. Yup. Good ol' dandelions. (You might know where to find some of those, right?) You can eat all parts of the plant: leaves, flowers, root. The leaves when young and tender make nice salads. Older leaves can be cooked and eaten. The flowers can be added to salads or dipped in batter and fried, and the dried roots are often used as a coffee substitute. The list of medicinal properties goes on and on—just look it up. Lots of possibilities. Your neighbors might even be happy to let your children forage the dandelions in their yards! A good resource is *The Forager's Harvest: A Guide to Identifying, Harvesting, and Preparing Wild Edible Plants* by Samuel Thayer.

What safety standards apply to the natural playscape?

Most North American states and provinces have safety guidelines for child care and school playgrounds that look to the national guidelines for their model. In the United States, ASTM specifies playground performance and safety standards and the Consumer Product Safety Commission (CPSC) issues playground safety guidelines (see the Resources section of this book). In Canada, they have Certified Playground Safety Inspector training and guidance. The CPSC guidelines are pretty detailed, fairly straightforward, but mostly geared toward looking at fixed playground equipment, not natural playscapes. Which means that it is quite easy to make natural playscapes pass guidelines and keep them safe for your children. Some of the most important safety guideline considerations for natural playscapes are fall zones and safety surfacing around elevated play features such as boulders, treehouses, and climbing sculptures, and head entrapments in play architecture elements such as playhouses, bridges, or decks. Another resource to help you design and build your playscape is *Nature Play and Learning Places: Creating and Managing Places Where Children Engage with Nature* (see the Resources section). Three key topics addressed in depth are designing nature play and learning areas, managing nature play and learning areas, and risk management.

Expected costs of design/build, annual maintenance?

Every project is different with costs ranging all over the place. I've done small projects for $500, but I've heard of elaborate natural playgrounds costing over $600,000! As a rule of thumb, natural playscapes can cost the same as a traditional playground. My projects average $30,000 to $45,000 for a community-built play space. You can save money with volunteer construction labor and donated materials, of course! You can also build in phases over time. It's always a good idea to factor in extra money for maintenance and management of your playscape when you do your fund-raising. Some groups add an extra 10 to 20 percent of the cost of the project to put in savings to apply for ongoing costs. (This may include sand or wood-chip replenishment, adding new plants, plumbing, lawn mowing, pruning, and so on.) You may be someone who likes a tidy garden and wants the grass to be maintained and shrubs pruned. Or you may be someone who plants the stuff in the ground and lets it grow tangly and wild. These decisions make a difference to your ongoing costs. The choice is up to you! (Kids may not care either way, as long as they can have fun exploring, playing, and creating out there.)

Do sand areas attract cats? Are there ways to cover that are easy?
Yes, cats are often on the lookout for nice sandy places to poop, it's true. While I hold my fist in the air and say "children are more important than cat poop," and "if we don't have sand for fear of cat poop, the cat poop will have won," it's still a health issue and something we have to consider when we provide sand. Check with your state and local health and safety guidelines to see what their actual language is. Different places say different things. Many regulations state that sand needs to be covered. But check closely because some regulations say that only sandboxes of a certain small dimension need to be covered. Groups I work with usually fall into two categories: coverers and uncoverers. Some people work hard to keep their sand completely covered each night. Other groups work hard to scan the sand area every morning for cat poop and debris (as part of the typical daily playground visual safety inspection). They simply scoop out and dispose of any surprises they find. All groups change their sand from time to time, and it is always a good idea to have children wash their hands when they come in from the outdoors.

Things to consider when covering sand:

- Have a cover that is lightweight and easy for teachers to lift.
- Rather than a tarp that can get weighed down with water and dirt, select a fabric or mesh netting.
- Covers that let in water, air, and sunlight are best for the overall health and cleanliness of the sand.

Other ways to keep cats out of sand and gardens (as told to me by various child care providers and a quick search on wikiHOW):

- Plant potent-smelling plants that cats hate—such as *Coleus canina* (often called the "scaredy cat plant"), lavender, pennyroyal, geranium, and lemon thyme—around your sand areas.
- Use dried herbs or spray plant-based oils of those plants around your sand area if you don't want to actually plant the plants.
- Spread batches of human hair around your sand area. (Ew!)
- Place citrus peels around the perimeter of your sand spot. Or take it to the next level and make a mix of orange peels, coffee grounds, and cayenne pepper, and sprinkle that around.

- Install an ultrasonic device—when this detects motion, it emits a sound that cats hate (available commercially).
- Use a motion-activated air blaster (available commercially).
- Install a motion-activated sprinkler (my personal favorite concept because it's cartoonishly amusing). Hook a hose up to this device and when it detects motion, it squirts water.
- Plant catnip in areas well away from sand to attract cats to other areas of your yard—mints and honeysuckle can work too.
- Pour vinegar around the perimeter of your sand area and the perimeter of your yard.

And a quick shout-out to a social network group I'm involved in that came up with these clever solutions:

- I was told cinnamon. We tried it at the end of the season, so not sure if it worked or if it just froze and they didn't use it anymore.
- My dog . . . just saying.
- Tarp it when not in use.
- I spray Boundary from pet store in the spring and they never bother it, plus we have a fenced yard.
- Here's a great recipe that cats do not enjoy: For us (almost 10 years of a giant sandbox area—19 tons+), we make sure to play with vinegar and baking soda on a regular basis in the sand area! We have lots of cats in our neighborhood and have yet to have any issues in the sand.
- Coffee grounds.
- Fishing nets. They don't hold water and cats can't dig. It doesn't help to keep sand dry though.
- Tarp it. We used bamboo-type window blinds (which let water through between the slats), then just rolled it up to remove it.
- Here's a great idea—a hunting net secured with rocks in the corners! Water goes right through so it doesn't get heavy, but cats cannot get in.
- What we do here in Roseville, CA, is mix sand (60 percent) with screened topsoil (40 percent). Screening removes the twigs and leaves and such. The soil part of this mixture holds moisture, which cats hate! Now that we are in the midst of a multiyear drought, we (occasionally) have to turn a sprinkler on our sand hill as it starts to dry. This mixture hasn't failed us in many, many years.
- We mix one tablespoon tea tree oil with one teaspoon dish soap in a spray bottle and spray around the sand area and fence.
- If you live in rattlesnake country, moth balls help keep them away, too. I sprinkle them on the outside perimeter of our fence. Never knew they deterred cats, too.

How do we apply these ideas in an urban setting?

These kinds of nature play ideas can work in all types of settings and landscapes, all sizes and shapes. Urban settings are great places to bring in nature and play. You don't need big spaces to still do great things (or big budgets). You get to be creative! Even if it means wheel barrowing loads through your building to get to the playgrounds, you can bring in dirt, sand, wood chips, stumps, small trees, and sculpture. Have a loose parts area for construction and imaginative play. Plant gardens, raised beds are fun. Sand pit, playhouses, a place for art. You can make the most out of a small yard by spreading out and using all the corners for features like shrub hangouts or mud kitchens, or a music corner. Also think about using the fence for features. I've seen people use fences for hanging talk tubes, storage shelves, a chalkboard wall, an art wall, a ball-roll wall, or a water tube; you could have a balance beam, seating, or plantings along the fence.

How do we adjust the environment for infants, toddlers, preschoolers?

How does one adjust the beach? The woods? The meadow? Nature is good for all ages. What adjusts are the children and how they use it at different ages and developmental levels. You can scale the features to fit your age groups. Build things smaller for infants—small bumps for hills, ramps, slopes, and so on. Make sure all plants are safe for nibbling and chewing or out of reach. I think of a baby area as also being an adult area, so always think about the caregivers and how to help them feel comfortable out there as well. If the adults are comfortable, then they will be more likely to want to be outside and bring the children outside. So, that could mean soft grassy areas to put blankets on, glider benches or bench swings for adults and infants. Think about planting fragrant plants and flowers to create sensory moods in places for infants. Shade is important too—start planting those trees now!

Toddler spaces can be the next size up—I like to think of toddlers as miniexplorers traversing over your landscape, investigating, sizing everything up. Hills can get bigger, build pathways to follow, small steps with handrails. Definitely provide opportunities to explore water—even small trickles are great. Sound elements, outdoor instruments. Remember: things don't have to be big from an adult's perspective to be big and exciting for children. If a child is 3 feet tall and gets to stand on a 3-foot-high hill, that doubles her height! Gives her an adult's-eye view and vantage point! The same goes for "forests" of trees: a small clump of dwarf apple trees is enough to create a toddler woods, and a stand of sunflowers is a flower jungle! Put stepping-stones down and toddlers will follow them to see where they go. A set of stepping-stones says "come this way."

And for preschoolers, you can begin to get bigger and wilder. More loose parts for construction. Larger hills. Rocks and boulders can start to be carefully placed for climbing and sitting. Gardening is good for all ages. Caring for animals too! Preschoolers deserve giant sand areas and sand areas with water access too.

Not the norm I'm sure, but what about folks who have a huge yard? What are some basic must-have areas for kids?

Shape the land: build hills and valleys. How about a huge digging area? Water. A big construction zone with storage shed for tools and materials. A covered area or gazebo. Gardens. Chickens! Drums.

How can you play it safe with natural playscapes to keep licensing from freaking out?

If you can, invite licensors into your projects and ideas. Share books and articles with them to illustrate your philosophy and ideas about nature play. Work with them to help your dreams meet guidelines. Sometimes all it takes is a small design tweak to make a water feature or climbing wall pass guidelines—the best time to find that out is before you build it! Some feel better knowing you have a written supervision plan for riskier items like tree climbing or boulder jumping. Work with them as much as you can so that children get to do all the things you know are important. Licensors want that stuff too!

How about plants that are kid safe?

There are so many great plants to use in children's spaces. Especially safe plants are of course edible plants like vegetable plants. Then fruit trees. Lots of flowers and shrubs are safe too. Check out the books listed in the Resources section of this book. I recommend Robin Moore's *Plants for Play*.

How do you add water areas with safety in mind?

Your water feature doesn't have to be fancy—the important thing is simply that you have water for children to play with and explore. A hose hookup is a good start. Add a sprinkler or a kid-activated dog faucet. Farm pumps can be great—makes the children have to work for the water. Most of the rules and guidelines around water are to make sure you don't have standing water: a pool or pond that a child could fall into, and so on. So, don't let your water stand! Water troughs out of logs are great as well as flowing creeks of rocks, concrete, and marbles. You don't need gushes and gallons of water. Small trickles will do. Push-button "foot-wash stations" that you see at the beach can be installed in your yard and connected to your building's plumbing system.

What are the best woods to use for durability?

I like to use black locust—a super-dense wood that is rot resistant and long lasting. Cedars are good. Osage orange. White oak too. Check with local lumber yards or sawmills to find out what woods in your region would be best. I always try to stay away from pressure-treated wood if children are going to touch it or it's going near a food garden. If you are just using the wood for stumps, logs, seats, or loose parts it almost doesn't matter what kind of wood you use. Let it rot away and get more! A pine log can last for a year or two, then it becomes a science project to see what's growing in there.

How can you make a natural playscape on a low budget?

First of all, I say tap your local community resources and see what materials you can get for free or cheap: boulders from local creeks, scrap wood from local contractors, wood chips from your municipality, logs from local tree service folks or your department of public works. Make a wish list of all the local materials you can think of. Then make a list of local people you can ask for help. Do you know any plumbers, carpenters, artists, pavers, plant people that you could bring into your project? Ask for their help and feed them pizza! As far as design features go, remember, you don't have to go big and fancy! Yes, it's true: a dump load of topsoil will entertain your children for weeks, if not months, if not for all time. The same can go for a dump-truck-load of wood chips. Or a pickup-truck load! Ask for plant donations from friends and parents of your children.

Steps to a Community Build

☐ FORM AN EXCITED TEAM

☐ DREAM

☐ DRAW

☐ ASK FOR HELP

MATERIALS
LOGS
ROCKS
PLANTS
SAND

PEOPLE
PLUMBER
CARPENTER
ARTISTS

TOOLS
SHOVELS
RAKES
BACKHOE

☐ BUILD!

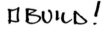

Resources

BOOKS

Banning, Wendy, and Ginny Sullivan. 2010. *Lens on Outdoor Learning.* St. Paul, MN: Redleaf Press.

Broda, Herbert W. 2011. *Moving the Classroom Outdoors: Schoolyard-Enhanced Learning in Action.* Portland, ME: Stenhouse.

Brown, Stuart L., and Christopher C. Vaughan. 2009. *Play: How It Shapes the Brain, Opens the Imagination, and Invigorates the Soul.* New York: Avery.

Bucklin-Sporer, Arden, and Rachel Kathleen Pringle. 2010. *How to Grow a School Garden: A Complete Guide for Parents and Teachers.* Portland, OR: Timber Press.

Carson, Rachel, and Charles Pratt. 1965. *The Sense of Wonder.* New York: Harper & Row.

Cross, Aerial. 2011. *Nature Sparks: Connecting Children's Learning to the Natural World.* St. Paul, MN: Redleaf Press.

Curtis, Deb, and Margie Carter. 2003. *Designs for Living and Learning: Transforming Early Childhood Environments.* St. Paul, MN: Redleaf Press.

Danks, Fiona, and Jo Schofield. 2007. *Nature's Playground: Activities, Crafts, and Games to Encourage Children to Get Outdoors.* Chicago: Chicago Review Press.

Danks, Sharon Gamson. 2010. *Asphalt to Ecosystems: Design Ideas for Schoolyard Transformation.* Oakland, CA: New Village Press.

Dannenmaier, Molly. 2008. *A Child's Garden: 60 Ideas to Make Any Garden Come Alive for Children.* Portland, OR: Timber Press.

DeViney, Jessica, et al. 2010. *Inspiring Spaces for Young Children.* Silver Spring, MD: Gryphon House.

Edwards, Carolyn, Lella Gandini, and George Forman eds. 2011. *The Hundred Languages of Children: The Reggio Emilia Experience in Transformation.* 3rd ed. Santa Barbara, CA: Greenwood.

Guinness, Bunny. 1996. *Creating a Family Garden: Magical Outdoor Spaces for All Ages.* New York: Abbeville Press.

Katz, Lilian G., Sylvia C. Chard, and Yvonne Kogan. 2014. *Engaging Children's Minds: The Project Approach.* 3rd ed. Santa Barbara, CA: Praeger.

Keeler, Rusty. 2008. *Natural Playscapes: Creating Outdoor Play Environments for the Soul.* Redmond, WA: Exchange Press.

Krezel, Cindy. 2007. *101 Kid-Friendly Plants: Fun Plants and Family Garden Projects.* Batavia, IL: Ball.

Louv, Richard. 2005. *Last Child in the Woods: Saving Our Children from Nature-Deficit Disorder.* Chapel Hill. NC: Algonquin Books.

Lovejoy, Sharon. 1999. *Roots, Shoots, Buckets, & Boots: Gardening Together with Children.* New York: Workman.

Lovejoy, Sharon. 2001. *Sunflower Houses: Garden Discoveries for Children of All Ages.* New York: Workman.

Moore, Robin C. 1993. *Plants for Play: A Plant Selection Guide for Children's Outdoor Environments.* Berkeley, CA: MIG Communications.

Moore, Robin C. 2014. *Nature Play and Learning Places: Creating and Managing Places Where Children Engage with Nature.* http://natureplayandlearningplaces.org/wp-content /uploads/2014/07/Nature-Play-Learning-Places_v1.0_Web_Sept-8.pdf

Moore, Robin C., and Herbert H. Wong. 2000. *Natural Learning: The Life History of an Environmental Schoolyard: Creating Environments for Rediscovering Nature's Way of Teaching.* Berkeley, CA: MIG Communications.

Nabhan, Gary Paul, and Stephen Trimble. 1994. *The Geography of Childhood: Why Children Need Wild Places.* Boston: Beacon Press.

Nelson, Eric M. 2012. *Cultivating Outdoor Classrooms: Designing and Implementing Child-Centered Learning Environments.* St. Paul, MN: Redleaf Press.

Sobel, David. 2011. *Wild Play: Parenting Adventures in the Great Outdoors.* San Francisco: Sierra Club Books.

Solomon, Susan G. 2014. *The Science of Play: How to Build Playgrounds That Enhance Children's Development.* Hanover: University Press of New England.

U.S. Consumer Product Safety Commission. 2010. *Public Playground Safety Handbook.* http://www.cpsc.gov/PageFiles/122149/325.pdf

Ward, Jennifer. 2008. *I Love Dirt!: 52 Activities to Help You and Your Kids Discover the Wonders of Nature.* Boston: Trumpeter.

Ward, Jennifer, and Susie Ghahremani. 2009. *Let's Go Outside!: Outdoor Activities and Projects to Get You and Your Kids Closer to Nature.* Boston: Trumpeter.

Warden, Claire. 2012. *The Potential of a Puddle: Creating Vision and Values for Outdoor Learning.* 2nd ed. Auchterarder: Mindstretchers.

Waters, Alice. 2008. *Edible Schoolyard: A Universal Idea.* San Francisco: Chronicle Books.

ORGANIZATIONS

The Alliance for Childhood

http://allianceforchildhood.org/

The Alliance for Childhood promotes policies and practices that support children's healthy development, love of learning, and joy in living.

The Children and Nature Network

http://www.childrenandnature.org/

Connects children, families, and communities to nature so children can play, learn, and grow.

Earthplay

www.earthplay.net

https://www.pinterest.com/earthplay/

Author Rusty Keeler's website offering resources, workshops, products, and design consulting services to help people plan, design, and build natural playscapes.

The Edible Schoolyard Project

http://edibleschoolyard.org/

The Edible Schoolyard Network connects educators around the world to build and share a K–12 edible education curriculum.

Evergreen

http://www.evergreen.ca

http://www.evergreen.ca/our-impact/children/greening-school-grounds/

Among other efforts, Evergreen helps schools create green school grounds and dynamic outdoor classrooms that provide students with a healthy place to play and learn.

The Free Play Network

http://www.freeplaynetwork.org.uk/index.html

The Free Play Network is a forum for sharing expertise and working together to promote free-play opportunities for children. Members work to counter the growing restrictions on children's play.

Kids Gardening

http://www.kidsgardening.org/

Kids Gardening and the National Gardening Association actively work with schools and communities across the country to provide educational resources and build gardens to promote health, wellness, and sustainability.

Learning through Landscapes

http://www.ltl.org.uk/

Learning through Landscapes helps children connect with nature, become more active, learn outdoors, develop social skills, and have fun.

National Association for the Education of Young Children (NAEYC)

http://www.naeyc.org/

NAEYC aims to promote high-quality early learning for all children, birth through age 8, by connecting practice, policy, and research.

The National Institute for Play

http://www.nifplay.org/

The National Institute for Play aims to unlock human potential through play in all stages of life using science to discover all that play has to teach us about transforming our world.

The Natural Learning Initiative

http://www.naturalearning.org/

The Natural Learning Initiative, a research and professional development unit at the College of Design, NC State University, Raleigh, N.C., promotes the importance of the natural environment in the daily experience of all children, through environmental design, action research, education, and dissemination of information.

Nature Works Everywhere

https://www.natureworkseverywhere.org/

This global program aims to help teachers, students, and families explore nature. Showing children how everything is connected reminds us all that we are a part of something bigger than ourselves!

Play England

http://www.playengland.org.uk/

Play England's vision is for England to be a country where everybody can fully enjoy their right to play throughout their childhood and teenage years.

Pop-Up Adventure Play

http://popupadventureplay.org/

The organization aims to support children's free play by disseminating information, consulting, and providing training to improve play opportunities.

BLOGS

Free-Range Kids

http://www.freerangekids.com/

Shares advice on raising safe, self-reliant children with less worry.

Let the Children Play

http://www.letthechildrenplay.net/

Promotes the importance of play in helping children discover their greatness.

Rusty Keeler's Earthplay Blog

http://blog.earthplay.net/

Author Rusty Keeler's look at nature play and playscapes.

Index